Acquainted with Grief

Acquainted with Grief

by
ADA CAMPBELL ROSE

THE WESTMINSTER PRESS
Philadelphia

ISBN 0-664-20949-1

Library of Congress Catalog Card No. 72-1408

Grateful acknowledgment is made to the following for permission to use their material:

Pearl S. Buck, for a prose quotation from her book *The Big Wave* (The John Day Company, Inc., 1947).

Norma Millay Ellis, for the poem by Edna St. Vincent Millay published in *Collected Poems* (Harper & Row, Publishers, Inc., 1954).

Mrs. A. M. Paton, for the prayer from Alan Paton, *Cry, the Beloved Country* (Charles Scribner's Sons, 1948).

Published by The Westminster Press ®
Philadelphia, Pennsylvania

PRINTED IN THE UNITED STATES OF AMERICA

Library of Congress Cataloging in Publication Data

Rose, Ada (Campbell) 1901–
  Acquainted with grief.

  1. Consolation. I. Title.
BV4905.2.R67   242'.4   72-1408
ISBN 0-664-20949-1

Contents

Foreword

Rarely is one privileged to experience at first hand the innermost being of another person. Most of those who possess the gift of conceptualizing the depths of their own emotions and the technical skill to express them would be unwilling; most of those few who would be willing are not sufficiently articulate.

Ada Campbell Rose is both articulate and highly motivated to share her story with us. As she says, "it has been my personal, irreconcilable grief which occasioned the writing of this book." She *had* to write this book; it was her pathway out of the empty wilderness in which she found herself following a shattering loss.

Clinical behavioral scientists will recognize the psychodynamic soundness of many of the insights Ada Rose has reached intuitively. Many of the specific, practical suggestions she makes have a universal psychological validity which makes them useful for any-

7

one who is groping for help in time of bereavement.

The authors of some books on death and grief try to handle the subject clinically, and therefore aseptically and at arm's length. Other authors cover primarily theological topics. Each of these approaches tends to be impersonal, whereas dying and grieving are the most personal of experiences. The bereaved who seek help need more than scientific explanations of their state of mind. They are in no mood to ponder mystical generalities. They need clear, direct guidance from someone who has been the route and has emerged.

Sharing even her dreams with us, Ada Rose has produced out of the crucible of an agonizing personal tragedy one of those rare, perfect gems of timeless beauty and utility.

WILLIAM P. CAMP, M.D.

Introduction

The writer of this small book has been motivated by an overwhelming need for reducing a Chaos of the mind, caused by grief, to some kind of Order. To a great degree, the work has fulfilled that purpose. In gratitude for the measure of relief that has been granted, even to a nonmystic who could not be consoled by those assurances customarily offered to bereaved persons, the experience is here shared with others who have lost loved ones and are seeking a way from darkness to light.

A large body of literature is already available for the comfort of grieving souls, and by finding the right book for any given reader's viewpoint, it is possible to help many persons who are in sorrow. For the bereaved intellectual reader, gifted poets and philosophers from all literary periods have produced words of beauty and sincerity which inspire response. Even in the field of hackneyed writing (which does not mean useless writing, merely nonliterary) one comes upon meaningful insights concerning the facing up to sorrow. There is, also, voluminous writing about grief for readers who have, or can go along with, some definite religious faith.

In general, people want to relieve suffering when they meet it at close range. Mankind is a kindly species, especially on an individual basis, but limited, and often we seem not to be made with the capacity for sharing the lowest depths of another's abyss. Friends—and writers—can call down words of love and encouragement but are unable to pull a victim up to a place where he can breathe more easily. The advice usually offered after other efforts have failed to comfort the aggrieved is, "You need time." But time is relative. "What you see, yet cannot see over, is as good as infinite," which means that the admonition to wait for help is not helpful to the brokenhearted.

This volume is addressed to grief-stricken persons who are feeling all but hopeless about recovering from the pain of sorrow, especially those who have not experienced some form of revealed religion. It is hoped that the book may also help persons who seek ways of comforting others—relatives, friends, doubting parishioners, or patients. It will be obvious to readers that the writer has no pedagogical, theological, or psychiatric claim to knowing absolute answers to problems of grief. The pages here are but a person-to-person communication, undertaken by one who has been deeply wounded by bereavement and would like to point out thought processes that might lead to some healing. There is no citing of specific procedures that are guaranteed to assuage sorrow, no promising that the sun will rise over dark horizons at a given moment. There is no surety that the burden of grief will be lifted by means which finally proved helpful to the writer; it is only hoped that the mutual search, between author and reader, for an understanding of sorrow may be beneficial.

We do not expect miracles when we encounter the nongrievous conditions of life. We know that love, for example, can be possessive or sordid—or it can be ennobling. We are learning that poverty, of itself, is not necessarily demeaning. Robert Frost, in fact, once paid tribute to economic deprivation by saying: "I'd hate to abolish poverty myself. Too much good has come of it." Indomitable spirits do not spring from prosperity; they are fired in other furnaces. Along with the variations of "good" or "bad" manifestations of love, or special backgrounds, it is also evident that people are not uniform in their responses to success, which ruins some of its winners while inspiring others to greater effort.

Grief, too, is a circumstance the results of which appear in varied forms. But a study of it, especially for those bereaved who do not try to explain death, may perhaps illuminate sorrow and prevent it from becoming a destructive force.

I will put Chaos into fourteen lines
And keep him there; and let him thence escape
If he be lucky; let him twist, and ape
Flood, fire, and demon—his adroit designs
Will strain to nothing in the strict confines
Of this sweet Order, where, in pious rape,
I hold his essence and amorphous shape,
Till he with Order mingles and combines.
Past are the hours, the years, of our duress,
His arrogance, our awful servitude;
I have him. He is nothing more nor less
Than something simple not yet understood;
I shall not even force him to confess;
Or answer. I will only make him good.

—EDNA ST. VINCENT MILLAY

I

The Triangle

In a Quaker burying ground near a small meeting-house in New Jersey, three graves mark the corners of a triangular space the sides of which are perhaps thirty feet in length. What makes this tiny space special, in the midst of that grassy plain dotted with identical low markers, is that the three Friends there were all young adults who died within a few weeks of one another during the early-winter days of the same year.

The first death of those three was that of a young woman just turned thirty, who had completed her medical education and had started a practice when she was struck down by cancer. My two sons happened to attend her Quaker meeting on the Sunday following her death and told about hearing of it when they came home. We did not know the young physician, but we were deeply grieved.

The next of the triangle three to go was a bank officer. On his twenty-seventh birthday the bank was held up, and when the gunmen ran with the money, this young man ran after them. As he dashed through the doorway, local police arrived on the scene, and thinking that the pursuant was one of the holdup men making an escape, they shot him. He died almost immediately. My sons and I read about this catastrophe in the papers, and although we did not know anyone involved, we were greatly saddened.

In the third grave lie the ashes of the younger of those two sons. He had suffered a brain injury in a playground accident when he was eleven years old, lived for twenty-three years after that, hampered by lameness and by damage to the pituitary gland which caused unutterable fatigue. In the end he took his own life—after being in a minor automobile accident—unable any longer to cope with the frustrations brought on by his handicaps.

Two in November, one in December. Within six weeks' time these three young lives were ended. I do not know the families of the two whose graves, with that of my son, mark out the triangle, but somehow all three of these unfulfilled young folk are dear to me. In the fall I plant snowdrop bulbs near the three places, and early in the spring I go to look for the blossoms. At Easter time I put a pot of yellow tulips between the stones that carry the names of my son and his father. On Memorial Day I place a pink geranium in the hollow where the tulips have been; then

I go home and put a duplicate geranium near the dooryard, so that we share the bright blooms all summer. At Christmas there is a wreath. And on any of these occasions I stop at all three corners of the triangle, thinking of those other two families.

Some people never experience any compulsion to visit the graves of those they have lost. They say—quite rightly—that the earthly remains of a human body are unimportant. I wish that I could adopt that rationale, but I cannot. Since the moment when I kissed the bronze urn and saw it placed in its resting ground, I have had to go back; go back, to say good-by to my son again, and to mourn again for his two peers in death.

It is not intended that this book be a detailed chronicle of my son's particular struggle. There are other writings which approach the consideration of sorrow by acquainting readers with the clinical story of one deceased. Some of these books are exceedingly well written—as, John Gunther's *Death Be Not Proud*. Such accounts serve a useful purpose, and in all of them the authors' problems appear to be resolved. This book is based upon another concept. Instead of trying to show that sorrow is universal, and that recovery from grief may also be universal, this writer seeks to persuade herself, and perhaps other sad, stubborn souls, that some unknown growth may come through grief. Is it the ancient folk knowledge found

in "Beauty and the Beast," where the hideous creature assumes his princely mien only when the beauty
has learned to accept him and say, "Dear beast, I love
you"? Is it that the human spirit is meant to change
in the crucible of suffering?

❖❖❖

"What is death?" Kino asked.

"Death is the great gateway," Kino's father
said. His face was not at all sad. Instead, it was
quiet and happy.

"The gateway—where?" Kino asked again.

Kino's father smiled. "Can you remember when
you were born?"

Kino shook his head. "I was too small."

Kino's father laughed. "I remember very well.
Oh, how hard you thought it was to be born! You
cried and you screamed."

"Didn't I want to be born?" Kino asked. This
was very interesting to him.

"You did not," his father told him, smiling,
"You wanted to stay just where you were in the
warm, dark house of the unborn. But the time
came to be born, and the gate of life opened."

"Did I know it was the gate of life?" Kino
asked.

"You did not know anything about it and so
you were afraid of it," his father replied. "But see
how foolish you were! Here we were waiting for
you, your parents, already loving you and eager to

welcome you. And you have been very happy, haven't you?"

"Until the big wave came," Kino replied. "Now I am afraid again because of the death that the big wave brought."

"You are only afraid because you don't know anything about death," his father replied. "But someday you will wonder why you were afraid, even as today you wonder why you feared to be born."

—FROM *The Big Wave*, BY PEARL S. BUCK

II

"I Am Too Much Bereft"

Many of the observations made in this book will be as obvious as, "One feels better after a good sleep than one does during wakeful night hours when there seems to be no rest from sorrowful thoughts." The value of unremarkable statements about bereavement is that, to the grieving spirit, nothing is obvious except the darkness of the experience; everything seems negative, and in order to regain a capacity for facing life one must prod oneself, or be prodded, with reminders of a more positive outlook. The word "cliché" comes from the French, where it means a "negative" in the photographic process—the image recorded by a camera, where lights and shadows are reversed, and from which a "positive" print can be made. If the clichés in this writing serve the same purpose, they will not be without value.

Within this context it may be observed that human beings meet with numerous kinds of grief—not all of them occasioned by loss of loved ones through death. Grievous suffering of the most acute variety often comes through frustrating disappointment, failure, or humiliation. A psychiatrist might point out that these are emotional responses to demands we make *upon ourselves* and that what we must do to feel that "we shall overcome someday" is to modify those demands. If we can come to realize that it is not essential for a given goal to be reached, then it becomes possible to live with disappointment: the undeserved loss of a good job, a love affair ended by jilting, a marriage wrecked by our own or someone else's weaknesses, the failure of a child to give his family reason for boasting about him, the hopelessness of having a dear one metamorphosed by mental illness, or the disgrace of seeing a beloved relative at complete variance with society's codes. This book will deal mostly with the kind of grief that is occasioned by loss of loved ones through death, since that is the sorrow which brings us into sharpest confrontation with the ultimate mystery of our existence.

One aspect of bereavement not always considered is that there are degrees of grief, even within the experiences of one person. The death of an aged relative is seldom classified as tragic, and in our time of medical "victory" over numerous diseases, the loss of an elderly person often may be regarded as blessed release from a half-life of senility or total infirmity. This is not to say that families are immune to a sense of loss upon the death of older members; the breakup of familial bonds is universally painful. Nevertheless, most survivors recover quite reasonably from this kind of mourning.

Even when the loss is of a younger loved one, the ravages of grief may be somewhat mitigated if we are prepared for the loss. Life ceases to have its total value during long or extensive illness for young or old, and following a period of morbidity the gift of death may be gratefully accepted. Sudden death, on the other hand, adds an element of shock to the survivors' sorrow, doubling the intensity of the immediate pain experienced. In our present social order, with increasing numbers of traffic-accident disasters, almost everyone has undergone some measure of this kind of grief.

Death by suicide, in our Western culture, is one of the most difficult losses to be met. When we have loved someone dearly, it is crushing to feel that the object of our devotion did not want to live; the fact that our love was not enough to hold him is sad beyond measure.

In recent generations, war casualties have brought death to millions of families, and the frustration of survivors following the death of young men in military service is very great, often regarded as a complete waste of lives. Along with war, the modern sociological scene has set other deathtraps which keep families in mourning—abuse of drugs, alcoholism, crimes of violence. Surely the tragedy of losing a loved one to such social ills is even more grievous than the deaths once caused by plagues and scourges.

In addition to the greater degrees of grief caused by sudden deaths, suicides, and casualties of our faulty social system, there are more subtle factors which often accompany the irreversible parting of lives that have been intertwined. As one example, many find it hard to accept the discovery, after a death, that a relative, or friend, meant much more to them than could have been anticipated. There have been instances in which a person has relied upon a lost one for good cheer, or encouragement in difficult times, and has taken those benefits for granted until deprived of them. It may take quite a long while to recover from this kind of loss.

The death of a loved one brings to survivors a new awareness of the bonds that kept them together, and this is particularly true when those ties have been very close. Within family relationships, no one should feel that it was, or is, wrong to be more congenial with one sibling or parent or child than with another. It is not a matter of preference; it is just a matching of dispositions. The loss of a kindred spirit makes the world seem very empty.

Another type of bereavement especially hard to bear comes when one of two life partners is faced with the necessity of going on alone. Not all marriages fall within this area—even some highly successful partnerships have not been close; but where there are no missing ingredients, where husband and wife have worked together, played together, and lived together in harmony, the one left behind by the death of the other is truly no longer whole. It is a desolate, an almost desperate, feeling.

Dependence of one life partner on another sometimes develops through domination rather than through emotional ties, and this too can cause severe strain for a survivor. A husband may have had absolute charge of his and his wife's financial affairs, for example, so that if she lives after he is gone, she has no idea how to write a check or carry out the everyday details of management. Or what is a more common situation, a wife may have been so faithful in caring for household details that her death leaves the spouse unable to handle the routines of meal preparation, clothing purchases, laundry systems, and so forth. If there is no daughter or sister to assume the chores long performed by a helpmate, the dilemma of one bereaved can be pitiful.

Even greater than the dependencies created by emotional ties or management arrangements is that which occurs when one person has had constant need of care from another. To be deprived by death of one who has given such care, or *even more devastating, to be bereft of one who required the care,* is like being plunged into an atmosphere that contains no oxygen. The life of the bereaved under such circumstances seems to lose its own value.

It goes without saying that sorrow caused by death's intervention in a dependency relationship is an emotional, more than a physical, problem. The actual chores that go to make up a life of providing for someone else (or of having another person provide for one) usually can be performed by new helpers; for example, a man often can arrange to have his laundry and his meals looked after, following the death of a devoted wife. But arranging to have everyday needs provided for is not the main problem. The grief of one so bereft is caused by the fact that the laundry takes care of his clothes because it is paid to do so; and perhaps a daughter-in-law sees to his meals because she should. No one really cares anymore.

The deaths that bring about the most traumatic effects of all on survivors are perhaps those which finally come as crushing ends to mortals whose time on earth has been like an inexorable march toward ultimate tragedy. Greek dramatists, and some novelists, have observed such lives, in which a clock seems constantly to be ticking away hours that move toward inevitable disaster. In the studies of such lives, little is recorded regarding the shock to survivors when the final blow is struck.

When sorrow is marked by one of the greater degrees, it cannot be reckoned with on the same basis as that caused by "normal" patterns. It takes much more of the relied-upon time element to recover from such grief. And if by recovery it is meant that the bereaved can think of their losses without feeling lost, then some bereft hearts can never fully recover.

The only possible way for helping oneself under the more difficult kinds of grief is to try to *understand* the nature and cause of the pain. And surely the best way of helping others who are suffering from extreme degrees of sorrow is to recognize the difficulty of the situation. Counselors and friends who want to alleviate such sorrows sometimes feel that their efforts are totally ineffective. Nevertheless they should make clear that they are available to the bereaved on a standby basis. It is better to show a sorrowing mother that she may feel free to reach out at any time for companionship and comfort than it is to advise her to keep her chin up.

Death is the final mystery, and though it comes but once to an individual, the great enigma is faced a number of times by the average person who reaches maturity, through the loss of loved ones. For this reason most of us must find out eventually how to deal with our sorrows and the sorrows of others. We cannot explain death, but we can try to recognize our human responses to death. What we say or do for bereavement is of little consequence. The important thing is to learn to regard the death of someone we love without rancor even though, or perhaps because, we have no choice but to accept it.

By acceptance, we do not mean reconciliation, or a false persuasion that all becomes happier and better with the coming of death. We mean, instead, that it is possible for the bereaved to learn that some sorrow cannot be "shaken off," that it is futile to expect full recovery from one of the greater degrees of grief. If we regard adversity as a form of growth, then we should be able to accept sorrow for what it is—change in our lives, change that may prove to be more drastic than growth of the body or hair turning gray. After a deeply grievous sorrow, we may never again be "happy" in the way we were before.

The loss of my son after his long struggle was a shattering experience, and the grief remained unreasonably acute for a long, long time. I know now that I will never be "the same" as I was before his death, but I am at least beginning to know something about the causes of my situation. The ability to sort out reasons for my disconsolate state of mind has been slow in manifesting itself, the early phases of my grief having been marked by confused thinking and a feeling of utter hopelessness. Gradually, though, there has come some evaluation of the elements that make this sorrow so difficult to bear. Every person who has this battle to fight within himself will have different factors making up the total pattern of his grief; in my case, two major circumstances have contributed to the whole. In the first place, this second son happened to be the fulfillment of my greatest dream in life—to be the mother of a happy child or children. My first son, a darling boy, was the victim of my maternal anxiety (augmented by a medical fad prevailing in the pediatric profession during his babyhood—the "scientific" feeding procedures and nonloving technique of caring for infants). By the time this child was of school age it became apparent that along with the doctors whose advice I had slavishly followed, I had been mistaken in my attitudes toward the child, and we were not as happy together as we should have been. After that mistake, I was terribly eager to have another baby and do a better job. The second son was a perfect candidate for my new efforts, responding to his environment in countless ways that made him the joy of our household. Until the time of his accident and brain injury, he was filled with gaiety and enthusiasm for life. During the painful twenty-three years that followed, in all our efforts (including his own) to help him adjust to the transition from having everything to having nothing, the struggle was nothing less than Sisyphean, making his final suicide a catastrophe of climactic proportions.

There was a second circumstance that contributed

26

to my grief in addition to the history of this son's problem. It happened that he was "my" child genetically, and parents will all recognize that such a circumstance can contribute amazingly to the relationship between two family members. It is not that sons or daughters whose characteristics come from the other parent are any less loved; it is the simple fact that a parent finds it easier to understand a child whose reactions are similar to his own. My second son and I did not look alike, but we thought alike. The same jokes were funny to us, we felt close to the same friends, our struggles with his handicaps after the accident were identical.

These, then, were the specific causes of my inconsolable grief when the physical damage to my son's brain placed him beyond my power to help him any further. That he could no longer tolerate life made life all but intolerable to me too.

Recognizing these factors in the problem with which I was left did not come easily. As a matter of fact, there are probably other factors that will become evident to me eventually. But seeing the whole situation even this objectively has, at least, reduced some of my chaotic grief to orderly grief . . . and surely order is the basis of sanity.

From these findings, personal as they are, and never to be duplicated within someone else's sorrow, it would seem reasonable to conclude that anyone suffering from inconsolable sorrow might benefit from first realizing that there are degrees of grief. Some sorrows leave deeper scars than others. After accepting that premise, a person may keep himself from being destroyed by grief if he works toward understanding the circumstances that have contributed to his state of mind. And finally, he who can stop expecting to regain his old kind of happiness goes in the direction of building a new and different life for himself.

Suffering produces endurance, and endurance produces character, and character produces hope, and hope does not disappoint us.

—ROM. 5:3–5

III

"Clear-visioned
Though It Break You"

The problems of coping with grief must be relatively simple for those who feel sure that an Earthmaker or Creator of Universes takes care of individual souls, in this world and after they leave it. "I come from God, I belong to God, I return to God," declared Ignatius of Loyola. Believing that, how could anyone grieve for long? The person who has examined his heart and his intellect for answers to the Riddle of the Universe and has found positive conviction that there is a God who cares, that the spirit of man is given opportunity to continue after its earthly existence—such a person knows that all is well with his lost one, may even look forward to glad reunion with the beloved. "O thrice and four times blessed" are those to whom such sources of strength are available.

The religious environment in which I grew up was typical of my era and locale—self-assured, white, Anglo-Saxon Protestantism. This segment of American culture sprang, of course, from a more primitive church—along with Catholicism and other branches of Christianity, but all these denominations have had in common the basic premise of the resurrection. In a letter by Paul, most influential of the early Christian zealots, the attitude of the church toward death is made plain: "In a moment, in the twinkling of an eye . . . the trumpet shall sound, and the dead shall be raised incorruptible." And the promise most often referred to in Christian burial services is: "I go to prepare a place for you."

Christianity has been one of mankind's most inspired religions—right for its time and providing millions of persons with meaningful ways of life. So happy is the situation of sincere Christians that they generally long to share the glad tidings. Their missionary program extends itself around the globe through the ministry, social work, education, and inspirational writings that are almost inexhaustible.

A Christian who has lost loved ones through death may find hope and comfort within the church's great body of literature. To be sure, some of the written works in this area are extremely obscure and not useful to a layman unless he is helped by commentators who can act as interpreters between simple minds and scholarly ones. But along with the difficult writings, Christianity also has developed more popular approaches to its philosophy, ranging from the successfully socialistic principles of Mormonism, to the simplicity of Billy Graham ("the Bible *says*"), and the "positive" thinking of Mary Baker Eddy or Norman Vincent Peale. For any intellectual capacity, there is a Christian writing aimed at assurance for troubled souls.

The consolation of true belief is available not through the written word alone. All the arts have joined hands to celebrate the Christian revelations of mankind's destiny. Paintings that tell the Christmas story and the Easter story are universally appealing; music that lifts the spirit expresses itself in glorious oratorios, hymns, and spirituals.

The Christian solutions to problems of grief have been here referred to at some length because that happens to be a philosophy most familiar to me, but we know that men have developed other religions which, for them, are equally effective in calming troubled spirits. Some of the concepts have been activist in nature: do this or that and your problem will be solved. Other philosophies combine action (such as the admonition to be a good neighbor) with meditation and thought control. Religions developed in the Far East have been particularly efficacious in providing tranquillity of spirit. Christianity, though rising in the East, has made little use of spiritual withdrawal. Instead of encouraging adherents toward acceptance of fate, Christians have taught that *faith* is the ultimate answer to unanswerable questions. "Have faith!" these good friends cry. "Have faith, and sorrow cannot overcome you."

But there are those among us who find the assignment impossible. Being commanded to "have faith" is about the same as telling a brown-eyed person that what he must do is to "have blue eyes." The New Testament itself records a classic example of reaction to this religion's demand for faith. "Jesus said unto him, If thou canst believe, all things are possible. . . . And straightway the [*anguished*] father of the child cried out, and said with tears, Lord, I believe; *help thou mine unbelief.*"

At this point it is perhaps appropriate to review in brief the history of my own religious feelings. It has been my personal irreconcilable grief that occasioned the writing of this book, and contributing factors may clarify the scene.

The certainties of the environment in which my formative years were spent fell upon a child who was a normal product of her time. In the expanding, optimistic, purposeful world of a growing region, under the wide blue Colorado sky, security was felt to be available to all who worked for it, and religion was cut to fit the pattern. Personal philosophies, in that milieu, tended to develop along whatever lines contributed to that security. So, one accepted the beliefs and precepts of one's immediate forebears—without audible question and without criticism.

There are notable benefits which accrue from such unquestioned convictions. For one, it offers safe harbor from the stormy seas of doubt. When I was confronted by unreasonable dogma, up until I left the carefree plain of childhood and went over the stile of adolescence to stonier ground, my solution to concepts I could not understand was to tell myself, "It sounds funny, but these grown-ups must know what they are talking about." This was a consoling thought, but the assurance it brought could not last forever. Even the revered Great Teacher said, "Except a man be born again, he cannot see the kingdom of God"— and being born again can mean the eventual crystallization of teaching into personal conviction.

And so, in the naturally rebellious years of puberty, my serene days of trusting in others' faith came to an end. I could no longer take Communion, nor rise with a congregation and state that "I believe in the life everlasting." The questions would not go away, and the only answer I could muster was, *I don't know.* Thus into adulthood I had no choice but to develop an agnosticism which, though not comforting, was honest.

The word "agnostic" has a harsh sound, and often is regarded as a synonym for "atheist," although the two words stand for entirely different systems of thought. An atheist is one who denies the existence

33

of God, and the atheist is as certain of his conviction as any true believer. An agnostic, on the other hand, feels that the existence of God, along with divine care for mortals, is something man knows nothing about, with no chance in any foreseeable future of finding out. All mankind is made up of agnostics "in fact"; the difference between those of us who cannot feel positive about the unknown and those who have faith is that they are able to project their beliefs beyond the obvious. To the agnostic, "Man is without knowledge"; to the mystic, faith itself is a reality—"the *conviction* of things not seen."

In many cases the codes of behavior recommended by different religions are remarkably similar; indeed, the interpretations of these codes are even subject to change with the needs of men in keeping with environments and advancing eras. Obviously it is not so much *what* one believes that is important; what is important is that it is a basic need of most human beings to believe *something*.

The problem of the agnostic in establishing understanding between himself and his acquaintances is that most people regard an adherence to agnosticism as believing nothing, which is far from being the case. It is very likely that no specific belief is clung to more sincerely than the conviction that one does not know the answers to life's unanswered questions. There is no doubt whatsoever in the agnostic's *belief* that he is not endowed with the wisdom of universal knowledge. The difference between the agnostic and his faithful fellows is merely that he accepts the intellectual limitations imposed upon him.

Nowhere in the range of a mortal's experience is it more urgent for a person to hold a belief than in his confrontation with death through the loss of a loved one, because death dramatizes the ultimate mystery of existence and nonexistence. For those who "believe" in resurrection of the body, or in reincarnation, or some other answer to man's unanswered questions —their concern for departed loved ones must be eased immeasurably.

To be an agnostic is to inhabit a lonely realm at any time. Actually, one's only source of comfort under this circumstance is that derived from the company of other human beings who share the pain of living in an unexplained world. At times of grief, when one is torn asunder from a beloved person, the wish to know that the dear one is safe, the longing for reunion with him, is overwhelming.

Until the death of my second son, I was more or less able to put the ultimate mysteries out of my mind and go about my little earthly tasks, dwelling within the limitations of agnosticism. Even since he is gone, I am still unconcerned with my own future or nonfuture, still able to let the future or nonfuture of other loved ones go unresolved. But the long years of struggle before this son took himself out of the world were so closely shared between us that not knowing whether or not his spirit is gone forever can be almost unbearable.

Even in the depths of this kind of despair, one shred of genuine hope and consolation is available to a person who sees nothing when he looks through rose-colored glasses. For if there is one special attribute that may be claimed for agnosticism, it is humility, and from this viewpoint the true agnostic never feels that the happy issues of faith are totally impossible. According to the agnostic concept, man's purpose has not been revealed to him, but this does not necessarily mean that there is no purpose. The limits of the human mind are so confining that within our feeble comprehension *nothing is impossible.* No man-mind could have dreamed up gravity, or magnetism, or electricity, or the changing seasons, or the self-perpetuating species of this globe. So why should men be able to dream up a purpose of life or a "solution" to its ending?

Along with the principle of not ruling out the "miraculous," the very nature of agnosticism includes recognition of the fact that one's personal lack of experience with revelation is not necessarily applicable to all human beings. Moses may have received the tablets on Mt. Sinai; Jesus may have walked on the water; Joan of Arc may indeed have heard voices; Joseph Smith may have communicated with an angel

36

who identified himself as Moroni; Bernadette may have seen the Virgin in the grotto at Lourdes. But for me, it becomes more apparent every day that I "must face the mysteries of human destiny alone." I have heard no voices, received no tablets, been vouchsafed no revelations—perhaps because of natural limitations that fall within the sphere of my other characteristics. It would be ridiculous for me to feel that all individuals share my lack of talent in the matter of revealed religion, just as it would be foolish for one person to be persuaded that no one could set a decathlon record just because *he* happens to be rather poorly coordinated. On the other hand, it would be equally absurd for an individual to assume that visions will come to him if he perseveres in their pursuit, just because they came to some others.

An important consideration of religious development for an individual is that of differentiating between personal mystic experiences, such as those accorded to numerous mythological characters and also to Abraham, Paul, Muhammad, George Fox, etc., and *others' belief* in those experiences. It is not too hard to understand that a certain individual may be in tune with the universe to an extent that gives him rare visions, but why does such a person assume that everyone can, indeed must, be guided by his new sense of purpose? One cannot blame Joseph Smith for having his dream, or for wanting to share it, but how can millions of ordinary people develop explicit faith in the dream as an infallible chart for their own goals in life? One answer to this question surely has to be that, as a song has it, "faith is a lie that you believe." True believers are those who can avail themselves of a comforting viewpoint, and the rest of us can only envy them for the reassurance they realize. An agnostic is driven by his own honesty toward confessing that he does not share the revelations which bring the hope and joy of mysticism.

One of the significant differences between agnosticism and faithful belief, we might interject here, is that to acknowledge one's inability to know about God is a step that does not come in one of Paul's blinding flashes on the road to Damascus, nor does it materialize in a fateful "hour of decision"; rather, it is to take the only open door the agnostic finds in a long corridor of ways that are closed to him.

By gradually facing up to the fact that he does not understand the design of life, the agnostic avoids living in pretense, but he does not escape certain intuitive responses to the helpless condition he shares with all mankind. An English Free Churchman, Nathaniel Micklem, has written a book called A Religion for Agnostics (SCM Press, Ltd., London, 1965) which contains some interesting insights. (Incidentally, the title of this book can be deceiving, and I suspect it was deliberately worded with delusion in mind. A reader could expect such a title to serve as a heading for an outline of "religious" thoughts that could be accepted by nonbelievers, whereas the author's message turns out to be his conviction that *Christianity is the religion* which agnostics will find compatible if only they will listen to reason.) In spite of the ambiguous title, however, Dr. Micklem's book is sympathetic toward agnostics, and it includes some statements that are convincing, such as: man (as opposed to other species) "speculates, he dreams, he *prays*." Certainly this is true, even of nonbelievers. It is quite impossible for one suffering from anxiety not to cry out to the unknown, pleading for reassurance even while not expecting to receive it. There is a vast difference between an intuitive appeal to any Governing Force that may exist and believing that communication with that possible Force can be established. Praying, within this insubstantial framework, is rather like putting a letter into a bottle and casting it into the sea, but it seems to be a natural reflex.

As must any other system of religious thought, agnosticism must be flexible enough to accommodate the infinite variations of qualities and limitations adhering to its proponents. This kind of flexibility enables me, in the matter of prayer, to borrow from my childhood trust in the faith of those around me. Having no real confidence in my own instinctive petitions, I still find consolation in prayers of true believers.

A strange paradox that has accompanied my grief over the loss of my son is that *he* had a deep religious faith. From early childhood, even before the accident which incapacitated him, he had a strong feeling of communication with the unknown; he was attracted to religious thought, and tolerant of various beliefs— though firmly convinced in his own liberal way. During his long years of suffering, he insisted upon silent meditation before meals; he enjoyed thoughtful sermons in other people's churches and took great joy in his own Quaker meetings. Always an early riser, he spent a half hour every morning—including the last morning of his life—at devotions that consisted of reading, meditation, and prayer.

Five days before my dear one took the step that ended his struggle, this entry was written in the notes of a brief diary he kept: "We thank God that the happy solutions to our problems have already been achieved, and we wait in faith for these to be revealed to us." The next day, with the last hours of his endurance ticking away, he wrote again: "We are thanking God that the solutions to our problems are out there waiting for us."

And, finally, the suicide note that he left is a document of utmost faith, containing no complaint about this world, but giving only a bright forecast of one to come: *"Dear Mother—This is not the real world; I go* to become *a part of that world. See you there. Love, Mac."*

I am certain that as he lighted that terrible match which burned away his suffering, there was prayer on his lips. Surely goodness and mercy accompanied *him* —and if there is dwelling in the house of the Lord forever, he is there. Thus am I able to benefit from his belief, in spite of my own lack of faith.

> *It had long been my conviction that faith had never been as creative a force in human culture as doubt and skepticism and the humble search for approximate evidence.*
>
> —LAWRENCE S. KUBIE, M.D.

IV

Sorrow Leaves Its Mark

The first days of living with the death of a loved one usually are gone through in a trancelike state. Nature appears to have provided a kind of shock absorber that operates automatically under severe strain. The arranging of a memorial service, the responsibilities of providing for solicitous friends and relatives, the satisfying of various legal requirements—these details usually can be managed while the bereaved is still in trauma. If the sorrowing one becomes really incapacitated, someone else will come to the rescue, for death, besides being the great leveler, is also the great creator of compassion.

The only people known to take advantage of grief are some funeral directors who reach into the sorrow of survivors with their greedy, sanctimonious hands and extract nefarious profits. Disclosures of the methods used by these ghouls are especially well defined in Jessica Mitford's book *The American Way of Death*, and concerned friends can be of real service to survivors by helping with funeral arrangements and providing protection against exploitation.

Unhappily, the psychological mechanism that protects one in the early stages of sorrow is temporary, and eventually the full impact of bereavement is felt. When the memorial service is over and the flowers have faded, the sorrow becomes acute. After the relatives have flown back to their homes, and the notes of sympathy have been acknowledged, when the door closes on the last visitor, and the empty rooms echo with overwhelming loneliness, those who have been left behind must begin to find their way on unknown trails.

It is then that a bereaved person comes to realize that never again will he be able to share some insignificant experience over which he and his lost one may laugh or sigh together. "Did you know that the quiet little lunch counter we liked so much has been closed?" "They are building a new approach to the green bridge we sometimes take when we go across the river. Have you seen it?" "Guess what—the bank is now giving parking tokens whenever we transact business there!" A myriad trivial happenings of daily life that have been important only because they could be understandingly shared now assume their relative unimportance, casting a veil of insignificance on life as a whole. This deprivation of the sharing way of life, added to the cessation of small rituals of love—such as calling "good night" up the stairs in given phrases—these losses create a vacuum that never can be filled.

Equally painful, in the early days of being without one's beloved, is the necessity for disposing of clothes that once covered the dear familiar shape. In this task I remember feeling compelled to kiss a pair of my son's shoes before giving them away. I knew it was a foolish thing to do, but they were his shoes—his shoes!

Small treasures that belonged to the lost one bring about daily emotional crises. I still have not been able to think of anyone who will take "good enough care" of the transistor radio my son bought shortly before his death, or the box of silver dollars he collected over a period of years. We often say of material stuff that "you can't take it with you," but we do not realize until we are faced with the situation that someone else still has to keep the residue of our pitiful worldly enthusiasms.

Perhaps the most grievous of all the immediate sad duties to be carried out by survivors is the collecting of funds from joint bank accounts and insurance policies. In the course of "normal" grief, being the beneficiary of a loved one's provisions not only can be accepted, but even can be enjoyed: "he would like it if I bought a new car, or took a trip." But when sorrow is of great degree, money left for the one bereaved is unutterably terrible.

As the long days wear on, many react to grief with a bleak and lonely observation of anniversaries, festivals, and special occasions formerly shared with the one now gone. The coming and going of seasons—especially the burgeoning of springtime—bring tears where joy once blossomed. As Shelley wrote in "Adonais," his memorial to Keats:

> *Ah woe is me! Winter is come and gone,*
> *But grief returns with the revolving year.*

The difficulty of living through the first year of a great bereavement is that familiar dates bring fresh grief. People of the Jewish faith recognize the importance of such a pattern by waiting for the anniversary date before erecting a permanent monument in memory of the loved one. In many cases, survivors feel great relief when they have succeeded in conquering their feelings at the end of that first year; it is only the sorrows of greater degree that are not mitigated by a complete turning of the celestial calendar.

In a newspaper column during recent months there appeared a letter from a sorrowing mother to the doctor who conducts a department of advice to readers. The mother wrote: "I lost a son over a year ago, and I can't get him out of my mind. He is always in front of me. Doctor, please tell me what to do." The doctor replied, in his kindly but impotent way: "Who am I to say, 'It's time to stop worrying about what has been'? I can't utter such banalities. I can only add this one—time cures, but leaves a scar." Reading that column, I wished that I could take the mother's hand and cry with her.

A common symptom of sorrow, according to the psychoanalytic literature, is the taking on of something of the specific problems experienced by the deceased. This has happened to me. My son was noticeably lame after his childhood accident, having a "drop foot" that he had to drag after the foot that was not affected by the brain hemorrhage. Since his death—although I am neither visibly nor consciously lame—I have to get tips on all my shoes because I wear down the front edge of the soles by a dragging of the feet.

There is no question that the manifestations of grief are different with different individuals, and I can describe only my own. Among these is the fact that I can hardly bear many of the experiences that formerly brought me great happiness through perception of beauty. A spectacular sunset—always a source of joy—now encompasses me with sorrow. Beautiful music tears me to pieces. A mother bird feeding her young fills me with a feeling of desolation.

My son's death has brought one result that probably is fairly unusual because of the special circumstances of his long unhappiness and eventual suicide. It is that I cannot endure even the simplest forms of suspense. I find it necessary to avoid news reports that are fraught with anxiety, such as the astronauts' lift-offs. An inconsequential buildup within a piece of fiction, or an unimportant bit of drama that is obviously a device for holding interest, where the reader or viewer is completely certain of satisfactory outcome— even these plot techniques fill me with such unbearable anxiety that I must put away the book or turn off the television set. Our long years of living on the edge of a volcano, always prepared for the worst, have taken a toll that seems to be permanent.

The most painful scar left on me by the loss of my son is the unrelenting tendency of my mind to relate *everything* to my memories of him. Take this typewriter. Before his death, when I sat down to it my first thoughts might be, Is the double-spacer in place? or, I need a new ribbon. Now, when I approach the typewriter I think, How many times he used it—very often doing a piece of work for me! What I see is no longer a typewriter, but his hands moving over the keys, somewhat clumsily, but with a sure perfectionist touch.

It is the same with almost everything I encounter. My son either saw a certain scene, or he never saw it; every object I touch is one he had or had not touched. The mantle of grief falls on every hour of the day and covers me while I sleep. Will it ever go away?

One avenue of relief that I seem to use instinctively —and imagine is used by many who suffer from sorrow

—is that of talking out loud to my darling. If I have lost my glasses, I say to *him*, "Where did I put them?" When I feel a stab of pain upon seeing the first daffodil of the spring I cry out to *him* about the discovery.

Many minds, under the stress of deep sorrow, are actually unbalanced for a time. The reactions to this condition are infinitely varied. In the old Norse tale of "Balder and the Mistletoe," Balder's wife, Nanna, was overcome "with stroke painless and swift" and was laid beside him on the ship that served as his funeral pyre. In our time, quite apart from the area of fiction based on universal suffering, we have seen Bishop James Pike driven to the occult in his desperate search for consolation over the suicide of a son. Lesser manifestations of grief may be observed in the unreasonable clinging to some possession of the deceased—a key case, a watch, or even a handkerchief.

My personal obsession, as a reaction to grief, was a necessity for getting rid of *things*. Household goods, many of my own little treasures, mementos of all kinds—nothing seemed of value anymore, or worth harboring. The Romans had a word for material possessions that describes everything I now own: "impedimenta." Never having been a dedicated "keeper" anyway, the few items I had kept over the years lost all their importance at the moment of Mac's death, and I have disposed of at least half the material possessions I had at the time.

Another of the ravages of grief visited upon many "left-behinders" is a state of exhaustion that takes great toll. Often one hears from the survivor, "I'm so tired, so tired!" It is well for everyone to realize that this fatigue is emotional in nature, more than physical, and can be dealt with only through understanding this fact.

One of the trials of sorrow that I have not encountered, but that often is undergone by bereaved souls, is a feeling of having been somehow selected for trouble. Why did this happen to me? Or, what have I done to earn this penance? Even Job, the classic example of endurance under grief, at one point protested that God "destroyed me on every side, and I am gone: and mine hope hath he removed like a tree." In defense of such paranoid responses to sorrow, it may be observed quite fairly that some people really do seem destined for severe testings of their endurance. Perhaps, like the "accident prone," there are individuals who are "trouble prone," for reasons beyond our ken. After all, a radio collects more dust than other pieces of furniture in the same room; perhaps some persons are "charged" in a way that attracts more sorrow—and probably more joy—than their phlegmatic fellows.

Although my own grief never has reduced me to a feeling of personal injury, an equally painful side effect of my suffering was a seeming inability to make any satisfactory recovery from despair. The question that kept recurring to me was, Why do I not become accustomed, if not reconciled, to my son's departure from a life he could no longer endure? No matter what had happened, or had not happened, to the bright spirit that came with him into this world, it would be unthinkable now that I would want him returned to the awful problems he had faced for so long. Why then could I not remember him in terms of his joyous childhood, or of those happy moments we managed to salvage from the wreckage after his accident? For a long time this question brought no answer, only a counterquestion: Was I clinging to my grief, not really *wanting* to be cured of it, because it replaced the anxious caring for my son that occupied my mind for the long years prior to his death?

Facing the finality of knowing that I could no longer help my loved one leads to another aspect of my grief—one, I believe, that is felt by many others who suffer from this kind of loneliness. It is the regret over moments in the past when I failed. It is not humanly possible to undergo a struggle as lengthy as the one I shared with my son without making some mistakes, but the memory of those wrong turns has been very hard to bear. Psychiatrists are prone to label this kind of anguish as a "feeling of guilt"; in my view that is a misnomer, for I am convinced that I never said anything to my poor lad, or launched upon any project in his behalf, unless it seemed at the time a way to help him. Even though I did not suffer from guilt, remorse over my mistakes proved acutely painful until I was vouchsafed an insight that has helped me greatly. It occurred to me one day as I was worrying over the memory of urging my son to look for a job—when he was much too tired to undertake job-hunting—and I wept with remembering my misguided effort. Then all at once I was overcome with the realization that he had made mistakes too, had sometimes hurt me as deeply as I must have hurt him. As an example, surely my talking to him about a job hunt that he could not manage was no worse for him than his final suicide has been for me. The wonderful thing about this intellection is that because I *understand* why he had to take his life there is no question about my "forgiving" him for the suffering that his suicide has caused me; therefore I can reasonably feel that he understood my errors, and readily "forgave" me for those mistakes which I made throughout the years after his accident.

The relief that has come with this understanding has been permanent and very real, serving me well whenever I am reminded of past moments that are colored by regret. Through this objective view of our mutual love, an "ocean of darkness" has been overcome by an "ocean of light."

❖❖❖

Grief fills the room up of my absent child,
Lies in his bed, walks up and down with me,
Puts on his pretty looks, repeats his words,
Remembers me of all his gracious parts,
Stuffs out his vacant garments with his form.
—SHAKESPEARE, *King John*, Act III, scene 4

V

"We Are Such Stuff
as Dreams Are Made On"

It is likely that one of the most universal responses to grief is that which comes in dreams wherein a lost love is brought back. Dreams have been fascinating to mankind throughout the generations, as far back as we have recorded history, and so most certainly before that. In Judeo-Christian literature, the Old Testament describes a wonderful dream wherein Jacob saw a ladder reaching from earth to heaven, "the angels of God ascending and descending on it"; at the top of the ladder, God himself spoke, promising Jacob that he should father a mighty people. The dreams of Joseph, along with his interpretations of dreams experienced by others, make up an important part of Jewish history as it is available to us in the book of Genesis. The New Testament, written much later, includes the dream of another Joseph which led him to save Mary and the Christ-child after the birth at Bethlehem: "The angel of the Lord appeareth to Joseph in a dream, saying, Arise, and take the young child and his mother, and flee into Egypt."

In modern thought, dominated largely by scientific viewpoints, dreams have been regarded as significant clues to human behavior. Sigmund Freud held that dreams reveal wishes and fears within the subconscious; since his time psychologists have continued to study the misty dreamworld in an effort to penetrate ways by which the human mind works. Occultists of various kinds have long looked upon dreams as evidence of communication between this existence and the unknown.

Even if we assume that dreams are woven just from memories, a vision—hazy or clear—of one who has died can be important to survivors. Dreams that I have had about my son since his death have been a comfort to me, and they have come when I needed them, occurring less frequently as the pain of losing him finally becomes dulled with time. I have seen him in dreams as he was in several of his "ages," both before and after the fateful injury to his brain—though never in his babyhood, perhaps because I require no imaginary reminders of that time. The wonderful memories of his happiness as an infant, and of my own ecstasy in caring for him, are imprinted indelibly on my whole being.

It might be useful in the process of tracing my illness as a grieving mother to relate some of the dreams about Mac that have come to me—not in the order of their occurrence, but as they showed him from early childhood to the time of his death; some of them, as may be seen, have even projected visions of him in a condition that we kept working for but never achieved. The reason I am able to report these dreams is that I made a practice of recording them, so that they would not drift away. At times I have risen from bed in the night hours to jot down details of a dream, in order not to lose it. At the time most of these dreams were chronicled I had not thought of writing about grief as a possible way of coping with it; my effort to keep the visions from vanishing was merely one of holding on to any remaining shred of those years we had together.

✧✧✧ Fourteen months after my son's death I had a quite clear dream in which I saw him as a little boy— maybe five years old (when he was such a gay little creature). In this dream he was on a tricycle and had hitched it to a small wagon in which he was giving a ride to a little girl younger than he was—perhaps three. She was "dressed up" with a big afghan wrapped around her tiny figure, and the two of them were playing very happily. Mac was working hard at pulling the wagon, being very "big" and masculine; she was accepting the service graciously and enjoying it as much as the actual ride. I was in this picture too—darting around trying to get a snapshot of the scene.

This dream doubtless harks back to one of the few times in my own life when I seemed to possess some strong extrasensory perception—an incident that did indeed involve Mac at four years of age and a little girl who lived next door to us. The two children were playing together outdoors and I was working at my desk in the house when suddenly I became aware of the fact that I had not heard their voices for some time. Where were they? I had a strong feeling that was as sharp as my awareness of the children's absence, that I must go look for them at a certain place along a rocky creek which was two blocks away from our house. I didn't question my urge to go there. Our car was in the driveway and I drove immediately to the spot where I had been "directed." Sure enough, there was Mac standing on a big boulder in the middle of the creek, and on a huge adjacent stone our little neighbor—terribly frightened by the noisy stream and crying hard. I was able to follow along the stone foot-path quickly and swoop her into my arms; Mac was big enough to reach the embankment on his own.

Was this the scene re-created by my memory thirty years later? Probably. It is the only dream picture of his very early childhood that I have had since his death.

✦✦✦ It was some months after that vision of him as a four-year-old that he "came" to me during his high school age. In these first years of his convalescence he was severely disturbed much of the time, requiring from his father and me long hours of patient care. We had arranged our daily routines so that one of us could be with him at all times, day and night. The thinking and memory functions of his brain had not been injured by the hemorrhage, but the damage to his pituitary gland, along with the painful lameness, caused such excruciating fatigue that, even then, he had made one attempt to take his own life. In my dream I saw him at this pitiful time; he apparently had somehow been slightly hurt, and there was a big welt under one eye. I had his head cradled in my arms throughout the brief dream, trying to comfort him and at the same time thinking what I could do to alleviate his distress —get an ice pack on the bruise, fix a dish of ice cream for him, suggest a plan for some pleasant way we might spend the evening, etc. My poor baby—fourteen years old and unable to strike out for himself; too big to be making a fuss over a minor injury, but so deeply hurt inside!

❖❖❖ The most obvious evidence of my own condition after Mac's death came as a dream that was clear and unusually sharp in outline. It seemed that he, as a young grown-up, and his father and I were on our way home from somewhere via a local train that runs between the city and our suburb. We had a lot of luggage, and the train had stopped at our station. The two men had stepped off ahead of me while I was still on the railroad car, handing down bags and suitcases to them. But the conductor was in a hurry and, in the end, wouldn't wait—so I was left on the train, still with some of the impedimenta—having to go on while they made their way home!

I'm still going on, without them.

❖❖❖These visions of Mac did not come in the order being related here. But to follow his life chronology, the next age pictured for me was the "Mercedes period," when he managed to find some joy in his car. The dream seemed to be a long one; I felt that I was coming home in a car of my own when I heard a Mercedes beep and Mac came along, driving rather dashingly to a parking place near mine, in our driveway. After a vague interval we were in the house together, and, surprisingly, he had a towheaded little boy with him. In this dream Mac was entirely different from the way I had actually seen him as a man; he was very self-reliant and "in charge"—not too anxious to see me, just being a dutifully attentive son. His car had some kind of insignia on the door. We talked a little—about the racial problem (which he had been interested in), and about some of his friends. He was glad to hear that I had seen an old acquaintance of his at Friends meeting.

This dream was not made of memories; it was a new

Mac with a new little boy—of his own? The vision must have been fabricated from all the hopes I would have had for him if he had never been hurt, including independence and a slight condescension toward me.

❖❖❖ In my next "chronological" glimpse of Mac he was so like his father that I'm not sure which one of them was the subject of the dream; however, I had a sense of having been with Mac as I awakened. At the beginning of the dream I was driving along a very dark street in a storm. It was hard to see where I was going, and as there were people along the side of the road I was afraid of hitting someone. However, no accident occurred, and finally I pulled up in front of a car that had just parked ahead of me. Mac came out of that car—I think it was Mac—carrying a brown bag, which he gave to me. In the bag I found an assortment of fruit—grapes, oranges, etc. We were both happy and pleased with his "present" (that is the part of the dream which is so like his father—always one to bring home delightful small presents).

The consolation of this dream has been its reminder of the love between Mac and his father, which deepened immeasurably for both of them during the years between Mac's accident and the death of his father ten years later. Their care for each other, and their mutual looking after me, was not only dedicated, it also had a wonderful lack of total dependence, either one for the other. (In the days immediately following Mac's accident, it was his father who would take him out and play ball with him, could urge him to get on his bicycle and ride around the block. I couldn't even watch these hazardous ventures, but would have to go into the house.) When Mac's father died of cancer, his sons were saddened, but neither one felt cast adrift. In contrast, my own care for Mac never achieved this level; I was filled with fear for him, a feeling that undoubtedly transmitted itself to his own thinking. Is this a basic difference between two parents—the father courageous, and the mother constantly apprehensive?

Anyway, "they" had brought me a small gift of fruit in my dream, and I still retain the glowing happiness of knowing that "they" enjoyed the giving of it.

❖❖❖ In a dream that came more than a year after he was gone, I was close to him as he looked at the time of his death. He had grown to be a large man, like his father, and I had my arms around him—as I often had, because it helped him to be touched. We didn't talk at all in this dream, but I could feel his warm back. It was not a happy dream exactly, but when I woke up I was saying: "Mac, I touched you! I touched you!"

Surely this dream was fabricated of the feeling in my lonely, empty hands when he was no longer there in need of me.

❖❖❖There is a snapshot of Mac taken five months before his death in which he is standing near a Quaker meetinghouse; he had gone with a girl to meeting and dinner, on one of his few dates, and they had taken pictures of each other. The snapshots had been made from some distance in order to show the beautiful simplicity of the building, and so the figure of Mac is small. This is the way I saw him in the last dream I had which brought him back just as he was . . . far away, but standing in a characteristic pose.

It was Mac, a very real Mac, in that dream.

❖❖❖ The strangest dream I have had about him was the one that filled me with the most gratitude. It came to me on shipboard, following a trip I had made in a futile effort to forget my sorrow by surrounding myself with new scenes. On the return voyage—coming back to cope with my grief for better or for worse—I had this dream, waking from it with a feeling of such joy that I wrote at the end of its recording: "Thank you, Mac, for this happy vision of your fulfillment!"

In a way I hesitate to include this dream in the present account, because in it I was Mac's wife—and it would seem almost sacrilegious for some apostle of Freud to put an Oedipal interpretation on the healthy mother-and-son relationship that always existed between us. In spite of feeling sadly certain that professionals who know little about a mother's heart will see things which never were there in my "conjugal" dream, I found myself in this role vaguely perceiving that all was not going well with our relationship when he returned to me after a mysterious absence to confess that he had been to what he called a bordello. In the vision I reacted to his announcement with proper wifely indignation, and we went through a reasonable amount of bickering over the incident. But the great thing about the dream was that in spite of a certain remorse, he indicated throughout the discussion a definite sense of triumph and accomplishment . . . and that within myself, I was *glad* for him.

What a revealing picture this dream produced, after the years of my own despair over the fact that his poor injured manhood had made it impossible for him to live a normal, outgoing life . . .

✧✧✧ The last dream that brought Mac to me was only *about* him; he was not there. It was very hazy. I was searching frantically through some cartons, containing I know not what, trying to *find him* and feeling sure that he must be there somewhere. It was not the bodily Mac I was looking for . . . but an essence of his bright spirit.

In a dream, in a vision of the night,
When deep sleep falleth upon men,
In slumberings upon the bed;
Then he openeth the ears of men,
And sealeth their instruction.

                —JOB 33:15–16

❖   ❖   ❖

VI

"The Troubled Sea of the Mind"

Throughout the long years between my son's accident and his death I used to experience a strange fantasy that would come, not as a dream in sleep, but during wakeful hours of anxiety caused by the fact that we seemed to be making little or no progress in overcoming his frustrations. In the fantasy I could feel myself in the yards of a sailing ship, clinging to some lofty rigging during a severe storm, while my boy clung to a nearby part of the same reeling vessel. I would be calling out to him against the noise of the wind: "Hold on! Don't slip!" Up and down we would go with the crashing waves, in constant danger of being capsized.

This recurring imaginary scene is unexplainable in some ways, since I grew up on the prairies and had no background whatsoever of coping with the hazards of sea life. Lightning, floods, and twisters, yes—but not storms on the ocean. As for sea stories, I never enjoyed them.

After my son was gone, I was no longer visited by the storm-at-sea daymare. His precarious hold on life *had* slipped, or rather, in his unendurable fatigue he had let go deliberately. He was gone, and there was no need for me to be calling out to him. The tempest had subsided.

But although my ship now lay in calm, I certainly had lost my bearings. At such a time in the lives of believers, they have but to pray, "O Thou who lovest all that Thou hast made, keep my child under the guardianship of angels of light, and grant that we shall find each other in the realm of glory." What magnificent words—almost convincing through their sheer beauty, and how wonderful it must be if one can be consoled by them! But when they only echo across the chasms of honest skepticism, where does one turn in order to find the way back to purposeful living?

There are families. In my case, there is another son (handicapped, in another way from Mac, but very dear), and there was a brother—close companion of my growing-up years—who came from far away and stayed for a week after Mac's funeral service. Both returned then, as indeed they should, to their own lives. No one can expect another human being to assume one's sorrow in addition to his own problems.

There are friends, many of them fervently wishing that they could help. Some of the most sensitive among these friends will not even come to express their love because they are overcome by feelings of helplessness. Of those who come, some are clumsy in their efforts at providing comfort, perhaps trying the "keep your chin up" type of admonition that is so useless to a broken spirit. One is truly grateful for the empathy of all those who feel inadequate, and even for the affectionate overtures of those who happen to choose unhelpful words. The friends who prove most understanding usually are those who take the course of *just being there*, for, as a German proverb explains, "Shared joy is doubled; shared sorrow is divided in half."

Among the friends who have been especially comforting to me since the death of my son, I have found myself reaching out to those who knew him well enough to share my love for him. There is the one who once worked in the same office with Mac who often said to me while he was there, "I really love him." How grateful I am to her now for her perception. I take flowers to her whenever I can, and she knows why.

In this world which brings us together as human beings, it is the obligation of a person who is visited by grief to *receive* as fully as possible the loving concern of family and friends, even when the consolation they provide is made up of moments so fleeting that they seem almost meaningless. The valley of the shadow is a place from which one must find one's own way, but as members of the human family we are obligated to our fellow creatures to allow them to *try* to help us, remembering that they too are lonely.

> *Geteilte Freude ist doppelte Freude;*
> *Geteiltes Leid ist halbes Leid.*
> —GERMAN PROVERB

VII

"Love Is . . .
the Practice of Human Power"

Until recent times, the power of love has been suppressed in our Western culture by taboos of various kinds. For long years preceding our present series of generations, creative minds only were allowed, within given limits, to express love—through the arts. Persons without creative talent have *responded* to those pictures, to that literature, music, and dancing which gave heed to our universal need for one another—but usually have been unable to free themselves from a fear of love in their own lives.

Religion has acknowledged that love is more important to the human spirit than food, shelter, and other material benefits—but our religions have more often been dominated by "Thou shalt not" rather than "Thou shalt." The philosophies of Eastern thought have proved less apprehensive of love, less jealous of its power, than the Judeo-Christian ethic which, when Westernized, became fraught with repression.

68

As individuals within this Western environment, infinitesimal fragments of the human species that we are, we have reached longingly toward the creative concepts of love, but have been afraid to avail ourselves of it. We have read about love, sung its praises, admired its manifestations in art, but have shunned opening our lives to it as if it were some demonic force. And indeed it *is* as forceful as fire, as atomic energy—but not demonic. It is the one power we know that need not be a threat to us. That is not to say that love is all "good"; if it is of lasting value, it becomes one of life's greatest burdens, carrying with it terrifying responsibilities, the necessity for almost superhuman self-discipline—yes, and sorrow. Shallow thinkers are inclined to feel that the manifestation of love will solve all mankind's problems, overlooking the fact that in its wake come staggering new problems. Still, it is all we have to turn to, since the alternative to love is not hate, but desolate loneliness.

The potential of caring for others is nowhere more demonstrable than in its relationship to mourning. When one is beset by grief over the loss of a great love, the balm most effective in making the wounded whole is some other form of caring. Grief itself being evidence of our basic human loneliness, it follows "as the night the day" that some other love is the anodyne most likely to heal an aching heart. This does not mean that another son must be substituted for a lost son, another parent, or another mate, for a lost parent or mate. Love is not always made up of the same components, any more than two spectacular sunsets are made up of the same color combinations. For one who has lavished love on another and then has lost the object of his devotion, the sorrow can be mitigated only by surrender to someone or something else. How unfortunate is that person whose life has not included an opportunity for giving himself in service to anything except the deceased. Such a heart, turned in on itself after a major loss, must be impossible to heal in time of grief. Even those who have had practice in the art of giving of themselves do not find it easy to adapt the technique to grief's dark problem. Why? Probably, because of that fear of love which has been mentioned, the inhibitions of the culture that have developed within us an automatic tendency to run from others rather than toward them.

Those who face the mysteries of human destiny without the benefits of revealed religion may find it doubly difficult to turn to love as a means of alleviating grief, since one of the assumptions maintained by our society is that anything which religious persons have incorporated into their beliefs belongs to them alone. For example, those who believe categorically in the pronouncements of the apostle Paul assume that most of his concepts are not applicable to non-Christians. So widespread has this viewpoint become that even nonbelievers often are convinced of its validity. The challenge for those of us who do not always agree with Paul is that of recognizing within his philosophy values that are available to us as well as to those who apparently understand his "reasoning." Take love. It is not the exclusive property of a "faith-state," nor even the eminent domain of those flower children who currently are developing modern forms of religiosity. In grief, the capacity for loving can be rechanneled, notwithstanding your beliefs. You need not feel that Paul's *agapē* is denied you just because you do not share his kind of mysticism.

Quite beyond the fact that love has healing power, there is an affinity between love and grief that also makes it right for one who is bereaved to seek solace in devotion to someone or something outside himself. This close relationship between love and grief lies in the mystery with which both are endowed. We do not comprehend the meaning of grief, nor can we explain "where lies the secret that makes one hand the dearest of all." Who can unriddle that mystery?

It is, of course, easier for us to accept the enigma of love, with its satisfying aspects, than it is to be philosophical about grief, which is—for the agnostic— a complete burden.

When opening oneself to new fulfillment, one should be prepared for the impermanence of whatever restorative is found, since all love is characterized by its fragility. As with many other experiences that bring joy and beauty into our lives—the full-blown flower, the colors of a sunrise, the laughter of a child—a sharing of love's contentment always must be tempered with knowledge that it too is subject to change—brought on perhaps by death, or the lack of developing understanding, or impatience, or even by subtle erosion.

Actually, the ephemeral character of all bliss may be one of its very ingredients; the fact that a given happiness will not last forever may be the element which gives value to that joy. Otherwise, why would a real flower be so much better than its perfect but artificial counterpart?

It is not easy, in the depths of grievous despair, to recultivate a new receptivity to others. But those who seek to overcome the suffering of sorrow will be wise to open up their hearts as much as possible, to welcome the touch of hands, the flowing of trust and understanding. This working at the acceptance of love will prove beneficial not only to oneself but also to the giver, since grief is only a form of the loneliness shared by all mankind. "Let me seek not so much to be consoled as to console," Saint Francis of Assisi said, and surely would have been willing to add, "even in grief."

It probably is true that the healing power of love, to someone bereaved, is most effectively released through one-to-one relationships. Relating to a sister or a brother, husband or wife, daughter, son, lover, or friend with whom love may be shared freely and without price can enable the grieving soul to discover those combinations of strength and weakness between two persons which supplement each other and make a whole.

In specific ways, the kind of companionship needed by one bereft can offer new opportunity for saving up things to tell someone else, and for generating new purposes in the daily routine of living. If, in addition to the finding of understanding, interests can be shared with someone who is willing and able to "take charge" of anxious moments, the healing properties of congeniality are greatly enhanced. A conscientious nurse does not say to her patient, "Would you like some orange juice?" She says, "Here is your orange juice." A great deal is said and written in current problem-solving situations about self-determination, but these prevailing techniques are all but useless when applied to efforts toward relieving those bowed down by sorrow. It is someone who cares enough to appropriate the right and the responsibility of helping with decisions who can lift the spirits of the lonely-hearted.

Along with the actual strength that may be derived through the power of love in time of trouble, there is another benison accruing to the tie that binds—a quality emanating from the very experience of sorrow. Most of our earlier awareness of love is marked by ambition, and mingled with various forms of pride. Sometimes these initial motivations grow into deeper understanding between those who love each other, but very often the "first fine careless rapture" leads to some eventual disappointment. By way of contrast, love that springs forth in the midst of grief can be bestowed and received without any demand for, or expectation of, perfection. Love so given, with both hands, so to speak, accepts relationship with the beloved, scars and all, and carries with it a blessing that is akin to a laying on of hands. This is the love that "endureth all things," that helps to carry the burden of sorrow.

If Love should count you worthy, and should deign
One day to seek your door and be your guest,
Pause, ere you draw the bolt and bid him rest,
If in your old content you would remain,
For not alone he enters, in his train
Are angels of the mist, the lonely guest,
Dreams of the unfulfilled and unpossessed
And sorrow, and life's immemorial pain!
He wakes in you desires you never may forget.
He shows you stars you never saw before.
He makes you share with him, forevermore,
The burden of the world's divine regret.
How wise were you to open not, and yet
How poor if you should turn him from the door!

—SIDNEY LYSAGHT

VIII

Reentry

Granted that love in its infinite variations is the one power that is strong enough eventually to overcome the worst ravages of grief, and establishing the premise that love (Paul's *agapē*, or any other version of selfless outreach) is not the sole property of the "faith-state," it still must be conceded that a person under the weight of sorrow may be temporarily incapable of re-entering the world and of receiving the love he needs. That familiar phrase "You need time" is nowhere demonstrated more clearly than in the resistance to love which follows closely upon grievous shock.

Where, then, does one turn while waiting for time to elapse? A person suffering from the illness of grief must piece together whatever fragments of relief are vouchsafed him. The first proof that eventual meta-morphosis can take place within your character must come from whatever consideration you give to the plight of those who are grieved *for* you. This does not mean that your sorrow has to be hidden; actually it is essential to recovery that you be aware of the fact that your grief, no matter how great its degree, is shared by your family, by your friends, and by humanity.

Beyond determining that "we cannot stay amid the ruins," there is no special order in which relief measures should be taken; the essential thing is to keep trying. One helpful practice is that of conserving *any* manifestation of respite from grief which presents itself, allowing such moments to accumulate until at last they form a meaningful total. When, after endless days of heartache during which every single encounter is but a reminder of the loss suffered, there comes a moment when some fleeting memory brings with it a flash of gladness, seize upon *that memory* and make a special project of bringing it back to mind. On the whole, the consoling possibilities of memory to one bereaved are somewhat questionable, certainly during the earlier phases of grief. This is one of the areas of thought not always understood by friends who feel it is comforting to remind you that "you have your memories." You have them, indeed, but for a long time after the loss of a dear one the thoughts of your beloved and of times you had together are acutely painful, not consoling. There has been, however, another kind of recollection that has been helpful to me in coping with the loss of my son—and that is the remembering of the loving care that friends and members of the family gave him during his years of suffering. His father, his brother, and an aunt who was a part of our household—all gave such devotion to the task of helping Mac that their love supported me too. It seemed to me, even while it was all happening, that the heartache of these other dear ones was almost double my own suffering because, whereas my agony was focused on the wreckage to Mac's life, their concern was for Mac *and his mother*. There were years after the accident when one of us was always "on duty," and I think back with gratitude on the confidence with which we turned over the care of our poor lad from one pair of loving hands to another pair.

Eventually, even recollections of the one who is gone will begin to bring happiness. The first memory of my son that brought with it a glimmer of joy after his death related to a wonderful day in the midst of his struggle when he told me of a victorious feeling that had come to *him*. I had been away for four months—in an effort we were making to dissolve his dependence on my care—and we were both happy over our reunion. He had met me at the station, and when we were home, feasting our eyes on each other, he said: "While you were gone I was thinking of what we have been through, and I had a wonderful insight which showed me how *we have always tried to make things nice. And, by God, we have succeeded gloriously!*" Of course that day's feeling of achievement did

77

not last—but by guiding my thoughts back to that triumphant moment, I am able to see that all our efforts were not in vain. He won some of his battles, and I *will remember that*.

Another device for putting grief into perspective is that of seeking out activities at which one may be somewhat proficient, even if unimportantly so. A bereaved person who works well with tools should pursue his craft; one who plays the piano with passable skill should practice again. The undertaking that proved most beneficial to me, in the early, confused stages of grief over the death of my son, was that of working on some free-lance editing. With the pencil in my hand, and the analysis of the manuscript occupying my mind, I felt an old surge of confidence in what I was doing.

Still another aspect of building a program that is designed for overcoming grief is that of seeking out creative activities. Just keeping busy is important; looking for ways of reaching out to others is important; cultivating creative outlets is especially important. Anyone can "make" something—be it a garden, a bookcase, a dress, an apple pie, a poem, a painting, a song. The "creation" of something that is partly made up of oneself can help to restore that self-esteem which so often is lost to those bereaved.

Reading, for those who use books either for learning or for recreation, can be a major source of support in time of sorrow, and here, as in the matter of faith, one may benefit from any hopeful outlook, even if unable to join in the hope. Classic writings are filled with great thoughts on death, since that ultimate mystery by which life ends always has fascinated writers. Recent literature, too, includes voluminous material on sorrow from both scientific and religious study.

It is true that a large proportion of the *opera* on death and the dilemma of survivors is incomprehensible to anyone but the writers; but along with the works made up of philosophical and theological lingo are books that speak clearly to grief. Among these may be counted Alan Paton's *For You Departed*, a blessing to anyone in sorrow, whether the reader enjoys or does not enjoy the author's Christian viewpoint. Through his great gift for writing one *shares* Paton's compassion for the suffering experienced by his beloved, his own grief over losing her, his search for an understanding of the mystery of death, and his thankfulness when at last he wants to "live and move again." My own reading of *For You Departed* has shown me another aspect of sorrow, which is that someone else's thoughts can be more helpful than those drawn from one's own resources. In his book, Alan Paton cites any number of writers who spoke to his condition: C. S. Lewis, Vachel Lindsay, Francis of Assisi, Walt Whitman, and others. But nowhere does he quote from his own earlier works which contain, among other profound passages: "Do not pray for yourself, and do not pray to understand the ways of God. For they are a secret. Who knows what life is, for life is a secret. And why you go on, when it would seem better to die, that is a secret." These words from *Cry, the Beloved Country* have been of great help to me, but apparently were not recalled by the writer at his own time of crisis.

So, read. Poems, novels, accounts of others' losses, philosophy if you can find understandable works in that area—indeed almost anything. Cry out with Frigg, in Norse mythology, as she recalled the warning about her son's death: "The sun is gone! The spring is gone! Joy is gone! For Balder is dead, dead, dead!" Mourn with David: "O my son Absalom! . . . O Absalom, my son, my son!" Join in Shelley's memorial to Keats: "He has outsoared the shadow of our night; Envy and calumny and hate and pain, And that unrest which men miscall delight Can touch him not and torture not again." Recall with Alan Paton the years with his Dorrie.

Death and sorrow are universal; there will be healing in the tears you shed over books.

Clergymen and medical doctors are often called upon as counselors to those in mourning, and through the practice of counseling many of them become wise and skillful in offering aid, just as a priest can be helpful through the confessional—for, as was once pointed out to me by my older son, who is to know more about sin than someone who has heard the sins of many mortals?

In the modern world we have developed a combination physician and clergyman—the psychiatrist—whose methods of coping with mental turmoil are even more objective than those used in related professions. The psychiatrist concentrates on problem-solving that may be within the patient's capacities, never telling him what he "ought" to do. And therein lies his special value as a healer of anxiety.

One way of compensating for the loss of loved ones is that of working for, and making contributions to, agencies that offer relief to whatever kind of suffering brought about the death. Money or time given toward the solution of problems with which one identifies can be deeply satisfying as a memorial. Another transference of interest in a lost one to new channels may take place when a survivor is able to carry on with some project that appealed to the deceased. This can be especially true if the project is a "cause," since the general principle of aiding others in any possible way surely carries greater potential for forgetting oneself than any other mental maneuver. The new widow who makes a coffee cake for her neighbor's breakfast succeeds in spending the greater part of a day in thinking about someone else, and sleeps much better after such a day than if the hours were monopolized by tearful recollections of her beloved. A widower who offers baby-sitting services to young parents will find himself rewarded many times over by their gratitude. Actually, it is hardly possible to overemphasize the importance —nay, the necessity—of throwing oneself away on service projects during periods of mourning. I have been especially fortunate in having a hospital "job" that has returned to me a million times over the hours when I was permitted to work there as a volunteer.

Many people—in states of grief or otherwise—find a way to care about something outside themselves by looking after pets. A cat, dog, canary—any creature that needs care on a regular basis can provide comfort, companionship, and cheer, and also the necessity for *routine living*, which has great value when putting one's life in order.

Extensive travel has proved beneficial in numerous cases of depression caused by grief. Seeing new sights and meeting new people did not solve my own problem, but others have found it possible to "get away" in spirit.

A widow of my acquaintance found new purposes in her life by learning to drive a car, after having been driven around by her husband for forty years. Another friend discovered renewal through a series of lessons in ballroom dancing.

One of the very best places a person can go when trying to pick up the pieces of a life that seems irreparably broken is church—almost any church. An institution designed especially for bringing people together in a corporate search for nonmaterial values has something of hope in its very atmosphere, and there are few churches where one is unwelcome, no matter what one's personal beliefs happen to be. Since the loss of my son, I have obtained consolation from the healing services of an Episcopal church where men and women of faith gather in efforts to overcome tremendous difficulties through prayer and through the confidence of their leader. In some of his leaflets this great pastor has written that "an immense field of good lies open to the modern Christian church in the realm of psychotherapy based on corporate prayer with faith in the Divine Power." Even a person who is not fortunate enough to share this trust may find it comforting or, likewise, be helped by the majesty of the Catholic Mass; the joyousness of the Christian Science refusal to admit "error" into life; the quiet of a Quaker meeting; the discipline of a Jewish service; the participatory nature of the worship in black churches. All these approaches to man's need for seeking some strength beyond his own can be uplifting.

One basic principle seems to underlie many of these efforts toward overcoming sorrow; they involve *going places* rather than yielding to emotional exhaustion and becoming recluse. Going *anywhere* brings enough variation of environment to crowd out, at least temporarily, familiar scenes that are closely associated with loved ones no longer there. One of the benefits to be derived from going places is that this kind of activity often involves being outdoors—a healing milieu of itself. In making use of the nonconfining outdoors, one should follow a policy of going out no matter what the weather is. Driving a car has an additional curative property, that of the close attention required for actual operation of the vehicle.

Still another benefit accruing from a change of scene, either by way of extensive travel or the over-all plan of getting out whenever opportunity presents itself, comes from some dynamic force within mankind that responds to mere movement from one location to another. A person who hurries to his job in the morning usually is just as eager to go home the same day; most vacationers are as glad to return from the mountains or seashore as they were to start their journeys. Just *going* provides for most of us the illusion that things will be better in the next place.

Remembering, even in the midst of trouble, that friendship never should be a one-way street, a person burdened with sorrow should make sure that he contributes to his relationship with others while benefiting from their thoughtfulness. Granted that a man in need of his friends may find it somewhat harder to extend hospitality than a woman does, nevertheless it is true that asking someone to join one for a cup of coffee with some crackers and cheese is not impossible, even in limited masculine quarters. Any kind of "entertaining" not only keeps friendship on a mutual plane; it may often open doors for friends who are lonely but do not show it.

Among other small ways of trying to fill a life that now seems empty, there is that of trying to end each day with some *plan* for the next morning. "I will take a bus to the shopping center and look for a gift to send to Aunt Marion," might be a reasonable self-assignment. Going to sleep at night with a plan—any plan—for the day to come will ease the hours of sleep and also the awakening.

For letter writers, messages sent and received can have great therapeutic value during a period of mourning. Such communication with friends and relatives not only relieves loneliness; the writing also serves as a means for sorting out confused thoughts, in many cases clarifying them.

Sometimes it is possible to combine two of these small ways of coping with grief—such as obtaining a box at the post office instead of having mail delivered —thus creating a necessity for going someplace to pick up answers to letters one has written.

There are, frivolous though it sounds, "games" that one may play which will mollify the pangs of grief. One is that of recalling the faults of a loved one who has died. He was not perfect—no one is—and thinking of his failings can recall one's fondest memories.

As is true of the flaws of other human beings, the flaws in Mac's character were but the obverse of his virtues. A prime example of this was his inability to accept those limitations put upon him by the disaster of his accident, and that was an aspect, really, of the endearing quality that drove him always to strive to do everything just right. He was totally incapable of giving himself any leeway on performance. The "little" jobs we found for him filled him with impatience; he wanted responsibility. His lameness, brought on by the brain hemorrhage, was a source of constant pain, but a burden he never would admit; he refused to carry a cane, though its use would have helped him greatly, and would have been a signal to others to help him. The outstanding illustration of his refusal to compromise with fate was evident in his attitude toward girls. His longing for a satisfying love affair was all-encompassing; one of his last diary entries is: "Wish I had a girl whose hair I could fondle." But he never once considered looking for someone who also had a handicap and therefore needed *him*; he was interested only in the prettiest, loveliest of charmers.

My poor Mac, the imperfections made him better, in the way a handwoven fabric is more valuable because the thread is thicker here than there, or the pattern slightly unsymmetrical at given places. Perfection is mechanical; variations manifest creative development.

A "game" that need not be played solitarily is that of thinking about all the beloved friends and relatives whom one has lost through death and asking, "Of these who are gone, which one would you want to see first, given the opportunity to see them all?" This query brings some surprising answers. One older man replied to the question promptly and with conviction: "First of all I would want to find my twin sister, who died of diphtheria when we were seven years old. I think of her as continuing to grow as I have grown, and I long to see her."

In grieving about my son, I find it helpful to remember that the childhood accident that caused his suffering and death was no one's "fault." He and some friends were playing together quite casually on the school playground when another nice lad threw the ball that struck my boy on the temple, bringing about the hemorrhage that damaged his brain. Nothing rough or mean or unpleasant was going on when this happened, and it consoles me immeasurably to remember that the incident, tragic as it turned out to be, can be recalled without any resentment.

The sources of help that have been suggested here will seem pathetically hollow to those believers who rely on prayer and divine guidance, and the ideas shared are not offered with any assurance of their effectiveness in alleviating sorrow. They merely comprise a record of some efforts to answer as honestly as possible the questions: "O death, where is thy sting? O grave, where is thy victory?" For some of us the sting of death and the victory of the grave are fully present, as scars upon our hearts that will be there until we ourselves go to meet the vast unknown.

What is, in this book, claimed for the possible "remedies" is that a bereaved person, no matter how deeply hurt, will find compensation for his frail efforts at re-entry. Skills at rebuilding the fallen structure of life can be developed only through some kind of practice. Furthermore, it is not essential to the healing process that all the experiments toward overcoming sorrow should succeed. The wonderful thing about failure is that it succeeds. From the *effort* to grope one's way out of grief's dilemma can come some fundamental insights that eventually light the way.

Who, e'er aspiring, struggles on,
For him there is salvation.
—GOETHE

IX

Insights

Gradual discernments that bring some understanding of the nature of things are so uplifting that experiencing them must be very like "religious" revelations. Especially for those of us who have reason to feel that we are unable to penetrate the mysteries of life and death, the coming of even a small insight fills us with gratitude. A few such wondrous moments have come to me, out of the blue, in the course of my grief over the tragedy that ended my son's life.

One of the ideas that has proved comforting came to me while I was washing breakfast dishes, doubtless after a night of subconscious wondering why I longed so to feel that sometime I would see my son again, wholly recovered from his handicap and restored to the promising pattern of his early years. Since I could never be assured in my mind that such a reunion with him was to take place, why could I not relinquish the yearning for it to happen? As suddenly as the sun breaks over the horizon at morning time, it occurred to me—there with my hands in the dishpan—that even if death brings nothing but annihilation to the human spirit, I will at least be able to *join* Mac in annihilation! My spirit will no longer be "left behind"; oblivion is something that we can share.

Another of the insights that have come to me relates more closely to the specific circumstances of my own sorrow and doubtless developed from my reminiscing over his beautiful childhood. He happened to have been gaily adventurous—always ready for whatever the next day might bring. Before he was born I had no premonitions about his being a boy or a girl, of superior or average intelligence, physically strong or weak, but I did have a strong feeling that he was as eager to be born as I was to welcome him. (Even then, we seemed to be doing things together.) This proved to be true; the snapshots of his early years show a happy baby reaching out for his ball, a joyous one-year-old taking his first steps, a "here I come, world" expression on his face the day he started school. So, even after the brain injury that brought complete exhaustion to his very existence, the character trait of being ready to go must have been there when he died; the taking of his life could have been from willingness to face the new as much as from the fatigue of holding on to the old.

The thought pattern that has done the most to lift

me from complete despair over my son's death was created after many months of worrying about the fact that I seemed to be making no progress whatever in stemming the tide of grief. Try as I might to forget myself and my sorrow through reason or service to others, it seemed that I would never again be able to live constructively. The house where we had lived together during the last ten years of his life was empty and dreary, the edges of the stair carpet worn where his lame foot dragged over it; the maple tree that he had planted as a seedling, patting it into the ground, kept growing. But it appeared that my spirits would never soar again, over anything. Each day and each night was a time to be endured, not lived. All this seemed wrong to me—permanently wrong, and something that I should be able to correct.

In the midst of chiding myself for weakness, it finally occurred to me that what was "wrong" was not the failure to recover, but the very fact that I was demanding recovery of myself. As once expressed by a friend who had counseled many bereaved persons, "the ones I feel sorry for are those whose spirits are restored easily, for surely they have not experienced the depth of love which opens equal depths of sorrow."

And so, after months of anguish and worry over being unable to recapture my old attitudes toward life, suddenly I was able to tell myself, with finality, "I'm never going to get over this loss." With that conviction as a tool for dismantling old ideas that had pre-occupied my mind, I was able to make room for new concepts of living.

Perhaps the reason it had taken me so long to realize that my former self had perished with Mac was the traumatic experience of almost witnessing his suicide. On the day he set fire to himself, I had no warning that he had reached the ultimate despair. I was recovering from a bout with the flu, and was staying home from the job we shared. He kissed me good-by that morning and left the house in a routine way—or so it seemed to me. I did not know that he was taking with him the container of gasoline we kept in the garage. Actually, he went to work—for a half day, meticulously finishing a deadline task that we had been working on. Only then did he drive to a remote spot five miles from home, carefully placing his jacket and "good" winter hat on the back seat of the car before undertaking his terrible ritual. When he had endured the burning as long as he could, he apparently rolled on the snow-covered ground to put out the flames, and then was able to drive home. When I opened the door to him, he stood there like a great charred tree, saying, "I'm sorry."

He lived for a week after that, during which time his brother and I were allowed to see him, separately, for five minutes each day. His brother would go in first, and Mac would say to him, "Where's Mother?" When

I came, we spoke only of our love for each other. On the fifth day it was obvious that he had pneumonia and was dying. By the sixth day—which was Christmas—he did not know I was there. I was grateful that, in addition to carrying his old burden, he was not required to suffer further pain. His long struggle was over.

But my share in our twenty-three-year effort seemingly reached on to infinity. No wonder that it took so long for me to discover that I did not have to be— could never be—the same person I had been. Nothing so awful as this suicide ever had happened to my old self; now I was someone to whom it *had* happened.

I can hear murmurs of many dear friends who are true believers saying: "Except a man be born again, he cannot see the kingdom of God. . . . That which is born of the flesh is flesh; and that which is born of the Spirit is spirit." But I was not changing from flesh to spirit; I was moving bodily, from flesh to flesh. From now on, I would be Another Person.

How does an individual become someone else? First by giving up the pursuit of former reactions to life. In addition to the building up of different expectations and opening the door on new responses to both joy and disappointment, I determined to speed the process of creating a new person by altering my way of living wherever it could be done without sacrificing integrity. As one small change, I let my hair grow longer, after having worn it quite short for forty years. Had my hair been long, it would have been easy to start wearing it short.

I changed the kind of music to which, for years, I had turned, putting away the recordings of Bach and Beethoven. Indeed, it would have been wise to give up classical music at this time even if I were not seeking new viewpoints, since the wondrous harmonies of the great masters now made my aching heart hurt more. By cultivating the modern beat of the new generations, characterized by its relentless searching for greater values and more honesty, I found myself in tune with others' efforts toward outfacing frustration.

Another innovation that has proved especially helpful to me in the work of molding new concepts has been that of attending a serious class in the philosophy and appreciation of art. Of itself, art has been of little importance to me because I have no artistic talent of my own. However, in the sequestered atmosphere of this class there was something of the metamorphic quality found in religious services—a corporate sense of searching out nonmaterialistic values. I have learned in this class that chiaroscuro is important to painting, and important to life; shadows make the light meaningful. I have found that "distortion is necessary to design"—and surely, in the mysterious design of life, grief is only a distortion of what we call joy.

The more one thinks of changing oneself as a way

of coping with grief, the more it becomes apparent that the whole pattern of life is change. Many of the transformations that take place in our lives are so gradual that we are almost unaware of them; this is true of our growth from childhood to maturity, our deterioration from full capacity to old age, even true of our encounters with marriage and parenthood. The changes wrought by grief are unique only in that they are called forth suddenly. The greatest consolation to be derived from this experience comes from recognizing its necessity, and from realizing that in grief the process of changing from being one person to that of being another person will not be the last transformation in one's life. To be alive means being born again . . . and again, and again.

I have not "conquered" grief. I have not been vouchsafed an answer to my cry, "Where is Mac?" I know where the big square hands are, the poor lame foot, the long eyelashes, the dark hair that grew horizontally across the back of his head. But where is the bright spirit that he brought when he came into this world; where is the depth of spiritual growth, the longing for his own home and family, the gift for languages, the remarkable memory, the striving for perfection in every task undertaken? *Where are you, Mac?* I do not know. But I have been able to stem the tide of constant mourning—having learned that it is possible to be transformed, possible to find help through disciplined living, to find love in new places, and thus possible to gather strength for climbing whatever hills lie ahead.

When you have a great and difficult task, something perhaps almost impossible, if only you work a little at a time, without faith and without hope . . . the work will finish itself.

—ISAK DINESEN